Group Quilting for Celebration, Commemoration & Charity

Linda Chang Teufel

Editor in Chief: **Linda Chang Teufel**

Graphic Design & Illustration: **Kimberly Koloski**

Photographers: **Kimberly Koloski, Linda Chang Teufel, Victoria Rentel**
and others as specified

Stock photography(cover) & clip art: **©iStockphoto.com,**
©Jupiter Images

Copy editor: **Pat Radloff**

Library of Congress Control Number: 2008903513

Teufel, Linda Chang

Quilting Party!

      Group Quilting for Celebration, Commemoration & Charity

            1. Quilting

            2. Machine quilting

      I. Title

            ISBN# 978-0-9641201-3-6

Printed in Thailand

9   8   7   6   5   4   3   2   1

Dragon Threads Ltd.
Extraordinary Textile Arts Books
490 Tucker Drive
Worthington, OH 43085
www.dragonthreads.com

Table of Contents

Introduction

While watching a program of Alex Anderson's *Simply Quilts* one morning, I saw her guest, Kelly Monroe, making these wonderful group quilts. I'd seen this technique done by painting at my sons' school. The art teacher had a large photo that he divided and cut into smaller squares. Each student got one square that he had to enlarge by grid method onto a larger piece of paper. Then it was painted and the blocks were assembled on the hallway wall. So instantly I was enthralled with the idea of doing it by quilting!

I contacted Kelly a few days later to propose this book idea to her but as a mother of three young children with a thriving financial-planning business, she was too short on time and energy to add a book to her list of "things to do in a timely manner" and so she gave me permission to go forth with the book.

In this book you'll find everything you need to organize a group quilt for any reason. There are step-by-step instructions for organizing a group, gathering supplies, directions on the techniques for quilters and non-sewers, easy finishing methods and lots of ideas! Anyone can do it. All you need is a Director and some willing participants – no experience necessary!

This book was written and color coded for the Director's jobs (in blue) and the Participant's directions (in green) and the pages each will need. The director should be one who has knowledge of sewing and quilting and will probably be the one to finish the quilt or have someone to help with those duties.

One possibility is to have a Quilting Party! All the participants would get together in a large space and work on their blocks together. Quilters could help non-quilters. Fabric paints and markers could be on one table for those who would rather paint their block or who do not sew. People could bring fabrics to share.

Then, when each block is completed, perhaps another person could quilt it together with batting and backing. It could truly be a cooperative group project.

QUILT RETREAT PARTY!

The annual three-day retreat of Quintessential Quilters was where the first Quilting Party took place. We were in the large ballroom of a lodge in the woods where everyone could work at their own pace. I brought all the supplies and my scrap fabric box and others shared fabrics. We set up stations for paints, markers and the Paintstiks™ with a heat gun plugged in nearby.

There were ironing boards around the room and a large box of imported chocolate cookies on the table next to the water tanks!

As the blocks were finished, they were pinned on the wall in their proper position and by the end of the weekend we had two finished quilts. The blocks took between three and eight hours to finish.

This is such a talented group that they totally got involved with this challenge and used all the tools to paint, draw and fuse with Steam A Seam 2™. Some created string for the fishing nets, some stitched a net and it was fascinating to see what they came up with from my box of scraps!

The Autumn Mums quilt was done by a dozen long distance quilters called the Sew Sew Sisterhood. The Bouchard family lives in Vermont, New York, California and Pennsylvania and have been doing one quilt together a year for charity. They, too, graciously offered to be my test quilters. Long distance was no problem and e-mail made it so much easier to get the word out to all members.

Eight sixth-graders plus one mom worked on the Flamingos quilt. We were all in my kitchen with three other mothers helping out. The girls chose their own background fabrics. A work table was set up with paints, markers and Paintstiks™ and the girls adeptly mixed the paint to the coral flamingo color. Only one girl used fabric for an appliqué. There were blocks of backing fabric to which they signed their names and later I pieced them together for the quilt backing.

Why make a group quilt?

As the subtitle of this book says, the reasons to make a group quilt are:

CELEBRATION

Housewarming, birthday, adoption, wedding, graduation

COMMEMORATION

Anniversary—people, church, organization, retirement, trip or occasion

CHARITY

Fundraiser for school, church, animal shelter, auction, medical cause

OR JUST FOR FUN...

A guild project, retreat, cruise, senior activity, community center and then the finished quilt can be used for charity or to decorate the building.

It would be a fun activity at a family reunion, or school carnival.

L. Teufel

Ruth Magill

Carol Bouchard

Passion Flower

Original photo by Vikki Pignatelli

passion flower

QUILTED BY THE QUINTESSENTIAL QUILTERS

Top row: Joanne Purcell, Bernadette Demos, Vicky Zacharias, Wendy Bynner, Jayne Metcalf

Bottom row: Kathi Machle, Teri Tope, Mary McLoughlin, Vicki LaRoche, Padge Weait, Maureen McCormack

Kay Hoagland

Buoys

Original photo by Victoria Rentel

QUILTED BY THE QUINTESSENTIAL QUILTERS

Top row: Padge Weait, Sandy Overturf,
Sharon Faulkner, Joanne Purcell, Lisa Sellers-West

Bottom row: Evie Wilson, Brenda Cade,
Denise Buergel, Beckey McIntyre

Sandra Blusiewicz,
Mary Clark

Patricia Daugherty,
Maria Slayman

Autumn Mums

Original photo by Carol Bouchard

autumn mums

QUILTED BY THE SEW SEW SISTERHOOD

Deb Gallo

Kathleen Scully

Leslie Quick

Carol Bouchard

Brenda Singal

Colette
Varanouskous

Carol Herles

Jeb Bouchard

Louise Byron

Tammy Hall

Helen Bouchard

Flamingos

Original photo by
Vicki LaRoche

Quilted by the Sixth-Grade Girls Club

Top row: Alison Bleier, Anna Klompen, Katie Jones, Alice O'Grady, Marchelle O'Grady

Bottom row: Kelly Bleier, Emma Galasso, Kaeli Hughes, Elizabeth Green

Basic procedure checklist

GETTING STARTED

The first steps are choosing your photo and selecting your group. The purpose of the quilt or character of the group will determine which you do first. Your group may be one which prefers to choose the photo democratically. Or an executive decision may be more appropriate. Or the photo itself may create the urge to make a quilt. Thus, the order of the Director's first steps may vary slightly from that listed below.

Here is all it takes to get a group quilt going!

- ☐ Decide on your reason for making group quilt.
- ☐ Select the group.
- ☐ Choose the image.
- ☐ Set the deadline.
- ☐ Gather materials.
- ☐ Make the packets for participants and mail them.
- ☐ Make the quilt blocks.
- ☐ Make labels/backing.
- ☐ Quilt the block.
- ☐ Return the block to the director.
- ☐ Assemble the quilt.
- ☐ Make the rod pocket.
- ☐ Bind the quilt.

You're finished!

Don't forget to take a photo of the finished quilt to give to all the participants as a thank you.

All willing participants should be included in your group.

For an anniversary or birthday of an older relative, you'd want each family member represented.

The number of people would influence the number of pieces that you need to cut the photo into.

If there are a lot of people, you could cut up the photo into many squares and then make the finished quilt blocks smaller.

And, on the contrary, with only nine people and the image cut into nine squares, the quilt blocks could be larger blocks. See charts on page 25.

If you have too many people, some could pair up and work on a block together. One could do the appliqué while the other does the threadwork, embellishing or quilting through all the layers or make one block per family.

You could have one quilt for kids to do separately—a small one with supervision if there are lots of grandkids or a school group.

People who don't sew can be included too. They can draw, color in lines, paint on fabric...enlarge/trace and color with markers or paint with textile paints or use Paintstiks™.

QUILTERS

If there are some knowledgeable quilters, have them help you organize and direct the participants. Perhaps they could do their block at home later and just help the inexperienced ones at the party.

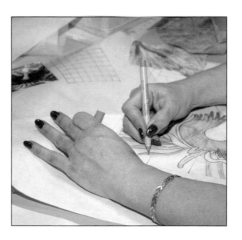

Ask if several quilters could help assemble and bind the quilt.

Choosing the quilt image

Carol Bouchard

Choosing the image depends on the intention of the quilt. Is this a gift for grandparents? Then it needs to be something personal and dear to them, possibly their home, garden or pet. Give it some hard thought and ask the participants for their input or suggestions. Here are some:

CELEBRATION

- portrait
- family crest
- prized possession/antique car, motorcycle, sailboat
- vacation photo
- a child's art piece
- pet

COMMEMORATION

- a building or house
- college team/sports team
- landmark of town, campus, state monument
- logo

CHARITY

If the quilt is for a fund raiser, consider what would appeal to the general public or your audience. It should be an image of common interest or popularity for the town or a symbolic item. Where I live, anything connected with college football, or their colors and symbols, would sell!

- something of general interest may be a garden shot, or an ocean view...

- Naturescapes—flowers, forest

- original artwork done by a child or a participant. Of course copyright laws protect art. You can replicate original art for personal use but not for sale or fund raising.

Look at the photo with an acetate grid-marked sheet over it and see if there are any blocks that would be a solid color such as a band of blue sky across the top or a band of black street across the bottom. That probably wouldn't be your best choice unless you want some easy blocks for non-quilters or children, or unless you must use that photo.

Carol Bouchard

Materials

FABRIC

Most quilts are made of cotton fabrics. There are many quilt stores where you can find thousands of bolts of fabrics of every conceivable color! But don't limit yourself to just quilt fabrics. Any of the fabrics in the Home Decorating department or fashion fabrics are probably suitable. If you need a certain color or texture try any fabric, especially if this is a wall hanging, where washing is not a concern.

Depending on the theme of this quilt and for whom it is intended, think about using:
- all the outgrown dresses of a little girl
- clothing from a deceased loved one
- silk neckties
- bedspreads
- curtains
- dishtowels
- handkerchiefs
- tablecloths

BATTING

Batting is the filler between the decorative quilt top and the backing fabric. It gives the quilt body and insulation thermal properties. It is made of cotton, polyester or a blend of both. There's also wool and silk but for this project, cotton or polyester, or a blend of both, is preferred. What's most important when selecting is the thickness of the batting. A thin layer is recommended, about the thickness of felt.

Batting comes in white, ecru or black. Use the color that is closest to your background fabric color. Generally you can use the whites for everything.

THREAD

There is a myriad of different types of thread on the market. Try to have a variety of colors and types for the participants to try. Variegated threads add a lot of color to the project and metallics add some pizzazz. It provides another design element in making your quilt block. See page 35, Quilting the block, for ideas.

FABRIC MARKERS

There are markers made specifically for fabric that are permanent. They come in thick, thin and chisel tips for all different effects. These would be easiest for the non-sewers and children. Markers are also great to add detail to the design such as eyes, shadows, fine lines, etc.

FABRIC PAINTS

Fabric paints are readily available in craft or fabric chain stores. Use paper plates or plastic bowls for palettes and easy clean up. Besides brushes of different sizes, you can use sponges or sponge tips on wood handles. Paintstiks™ are oil paint in a crayon form and very easy to use. Just draw and then follow instructions on how to use a heat tool to dry it, or simply air dry it for two days to set the paint.

STEAM-A-SEAM 2

Steam-A-Seam 2 is a fusible webbing that has adhesive on both sides under paper backing. Shapes will stick to backing temporarily and is permanent when fused with an iron. It's used for appliqué.

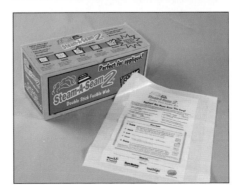

Finished quilt size

Now you must decide what you want the finished quilt size to be. I'd suggest the maximum size of the quilt block that I'd have a participant make would be 12" square (plus half inch seam allowances all around so cut size is 13").

For example, if you cut the photo into 24 squares (4 x 6) and each quilt fabric block finished size is 10" then the finished quilt would be 40" x 60".

If that's too large, then make each finished quilt block smaller. An 8" finished block would yield a quilt that is 32" x 48".

Example: You, or the participant, will cut out an 11"-square piece of background fabric and draw lines ½" around all sides for seam allowance. That means all the art must be done within the lines of the 10" square.

To mark the seam allowance there are special temporary fabric markers, such as water soluble markers, chalk, fabric pencils, but you can always use a light pencil line. Or, in your letter, instruct the quilter to use an 11" background fabric and mark the ½" seam allowance all around if you aren't sending fabric.

Dividing the photo

Take your master photo and enlarge it at a copy or photo store. A 35 mm negative can be enlarged to 8" x 12" or 11" x 14" without cropping. It can be made to 8" x 10" but then the image would be cropped. A digital can be made any size but some of the photo may be cropped also.

Important! Make two copies of the reference photo first and don't cut your original.

NOTE: You may want to crop the enlarged photo to a desired size to make it easier to divide or to only include certain parts of the photo. You must crop the photo before dividing. Make both copies the same.

Here is where you'll need to decide whether you will give every participant a small print of the entire photo or let them be surprised when they see it all put together.

A good suggested size to cut the photo would be no smaller than 2" squares.

For an 11" x 14" photo you may want to crop it so it can be cut into even squares as shown in the chart. Trim off top and/or bottom depending on the image.

As you can see, the size you enlarge the photo and the size of square you cut determines the number of blocks you need to make. If you have more participants than squares, perhaps two can work on one block (mother and child).

Example: A master photo of 9"x 12" can be cut into 3" squares to make 12 pieces or 12 quilt blocks.

MASTER PHOTO SIZE (inches)

CUT PHOTO SIZE (inches)	7½ x 10	8 x 12	9 x 9	9 x 12	10 x 14	10½ x 14
2		24			35	
2½	12					
3			9	12		
3½						12
4		6				

Dividing the photo

Once you've decided what size pieces to cut the photo, you need to carefully draw the grid line on the photo exactly where you want to cut it. The best way to cut it would be with a long ruler and an X-ACTO® knife.

1A	1B	1C	1D	1E
2A	2B	2C	2D	2E
3A	3B	3C	3D	3E
4A	4B	4C	4D	4E

After cutting, and before disturbing them from their original position, you'll need to number the back of the pieces.

Start from the top row, go across to the end and then down to the next row. Try not to turn them upside down when numbering.

Top row is #1 and then left to right is A, B, C and so on.

Next row is #2 and continue in this manner.

Now put one piece in each participant's bag as the sample they will replicate for their quilt block. Give each participant a sheet or two of acetate that is marked in permanent marker with the grid for the photo piece.

Also, you may want to record who has which piece such as: Sarah has 3-B, so if she loses it or can't complete it, you'll easily be able to get another photo piece.

When distributing these pieces to the quilters, you need to consider their skill level.

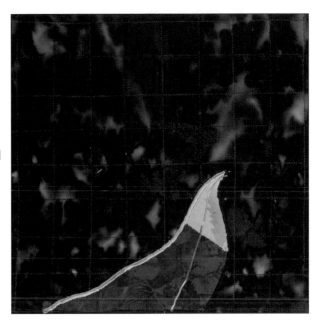

An easier piece with little detail should be given to a beginner. This block with the tip of a leaf was given to a beginner and she made an impressive block by choosing this black background fabric with mottled color in it and by the shading she did on the small leaf tip with a satin stitch.

This complex photo piece with a lot of detail was given to a professional quilter and she created this magnificent block!

Enlarging the photo

GRID METHOD

This grid method is an easy way to enlarge the image from the small photo square into a larger fabric block. The grid helps you look at the photo proportionally for placement of designs and easier transfer of lines.

Place your photo piece right side up.

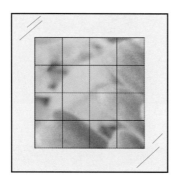

Place the clear acetate on top. With a fine permanent marker draw the outline of the perimeter of the photo.

Depending on the size of the photo, you need to divide it into an even grid. If it's a 2" square of photo, I'd make a ½-inch grid on the acetate.

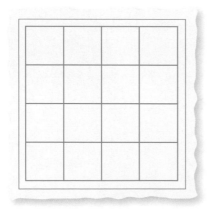

Onto a piece of paper draw the size of your finished block and then add a ½-inch seam allowance all around.

Now, disregard the seam allowances and work only within the inner block. Draw a matching grid with the same number of squares as the acetate but larger size squares.

The easiest way is to divide the inner block in half and then divide these two sections in half again.

Your block should look like this.

Now put the acetate grid covered reference photo next to the grid paper block. Look at one box of the photo grid at a time. Start at the top right corner photo box – see where the photo lines are near the drawn grid.

These need to be transposed to the same place on the paper grid.

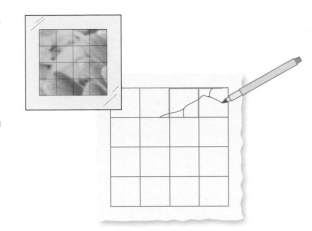

After you have it all drawn on paper, it should look like this.

Tape acetate sheet over it and trace with a permanent marker for your reference template.

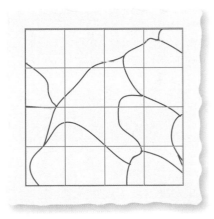

ALTERNATE METHOD:

COPY SHOP ENLARGING

The easiest way is to bring the photo square to a professional copy shop and have them enlarge it to the finished block size needed. They can do the calculation.

Also the photo piece can be scanned into your computer if you have a program that can print it to the larger size needed and then you can trace the design on the fabric or paper. See the formula at right.

FORMULA FOR ENLARGING A PHOTO

$$\text{Finished block size} \div \text{size of photo square} \times 100 = \% \text{ to enlarge}$$

For example: If the photo square is 2" and you'd like the quilt block to be 12" finished:

$$12 \div 2 \times 100 = 600\%$$

Making the Block

TRANSFERRING THE DESIGN TO FABRIC

FOR NON-QUILTERS:
If you don't want to sew the design, then at this point you can trace your design onto the fabric block and then use paint, markers or Paintstiks™ to fill it in.

To trace, tape your paper drawing or template and place on a light box or sunny window. Then tape the fabric square over it and draw the main lines onto the fabric using temporary fabric markers or pencil.

FOR QUILTERS:
Many different techniques can be used to apply your design to the fabric. Here are easy directions for raw edge fusing appliqué using a fusible web such as Steam-A-Seam 2™, but you may know other methods: freezer paper appliqué, reverse appliqué or needle-turned hand appliqué. Feel free to use any that are comfortable for you.

FUSING

Steam-A-Seam 2™ is a fusible web with pressure sensitive coating on both sides which allows for a temporary hold to both the appliqué and the background materials. Your entire appliqué stays in place without shifting or moving and it is repositionable until ironed.

Trace one of the shapes onto a piece of Steam-A-Seam 2™.

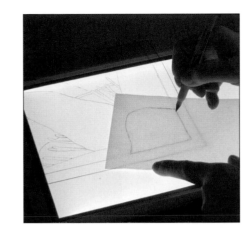

Peel off the backing without the drawing on it.

Stick the drawing to the wrong side of the desired fabric and cut exactly along the traced lines.

Peel off remaining paper and place on background in the correct position. To find the position- place the acetate on top of the background square box. Lift part of the acetate to slip the piece under it and in the right location and then press to adhere it.

Repeat until all the pieces are exactly positioned and then press with hot iron for 10-15 seconds.

Check to make sure edges are securely fused to background.

Making the Block

BASIC APPLIQUÉ

To prepare appliqué, see Fusing directions. When all pieces are in their final positions, you can appliqué to keep them permanently attached to the fabric allowing you to decorate the designs.

SATIN STITCHING:

On a scrap of fabric two layers thick, adjust zigzag to a width of between 1.8 and 2.5 and a stitch length of 0.3 – 0.5. Check the test swatch to see that it is a nice smooth zigzag where the stitches lay next to each other and form a solid bar of thread.

Place satin stitch on an appliqué piece so the left swing of the needle is on the piece and the right swing is just off the edge.

TO STITCH AN OUTSIDE ANGLE:

Stitch to end of piece and place needle down on right (outside)- just off the end of the fabric. Pivot and continue stitching with first few stitches overlapping.

PIVOT HERE

TO STITCH AN INSIDE ANGLE:

For the corner, stitch a few zigzags onto the appliqué piece to approximately the width of the zigzag and put the needle down on left (inside). Pivot and continue stitching with first few stitches overlapping.

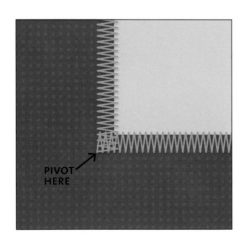

PIVOT HERE

To go around an outside curve:

Put needle down on the outside of piece and pivot slightly. Do this every few stitches for a smooth curve with no angles.

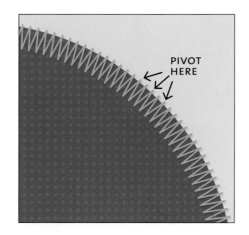

To go around an inside curve:

Put needle down on the inside of the piece and pivot. Pivot often for a smooth curve.

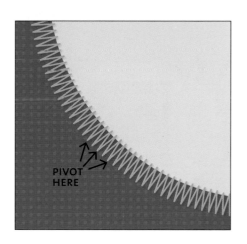

To sew points such as stars:

Satin stitch leg of star with stitch width of 2.5 until the left swing of needle goes across star leg. Narrow the stitch width and take a few stitches making sure not to swing over the left side. Narrow the stitch width again until almost straight and sew to the point. Stop with the needle in the fabric, pivot and sew a few more of these stitches, increase stitch width and take a few stitches. Increase stitch width to 2.5 and repeat around the star.

Straight stitch appliqué

Using a straight stitch you could stitch close to the cut edge of the appliqué with a decorative thread and a short stitch of about 2.0.

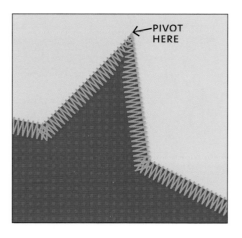

Finishing the Block

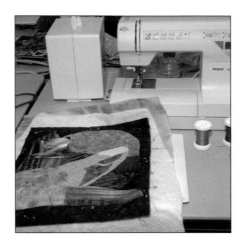

The first step is to layer the finished quilt block top with batting and then a piece of backing.

Cut both the batting and backing larger than the block, about 1" bigger all around. Pin all layers together so right side of backing is facing out.

Backing should be of a quilting cotton. (It may be provided in the kit.) Not all the backing fabric has to be the same. Consider a light fabric where the artist can sign and date the back with a permanent fabric marker.

LABEL ON BACKING

You could simply sign your name on the backing of the block as in the Flamingo quilt.

• Or write the purpose of this quilt...Mary & Bill's 50th anniversary.

• Or each family member can write a personal message on each block...Enjoy your retirement!

• Or add short poem on label.

If it's a dark fabric, you may need to sign on another piece of light fabric and then sew it to the backing by hand.

In addition to using markers or Paintstiks™ you could:

• embroider your name by hand or machine or free-motion stitch your name.

• print photo transfer of your message or a photo of yourself.

PHOTO TRANSFER

Wouldn't it be fun for a family quilt if everyone's face (or family photo) was on the back of each block?

Photo transfer fabric is available in quilting stores and feeds into the color printer of your computer. Scan in a photo or type your label and then print it onto this special fabric. Then, cut out the fabric and sew it onto the back of the block. You could print several photos/labels on one sheet and then cut them apart.

QUILTING THE BLOCK

After you pin the backing, batting and quilt top pieces together, there are options of how to quilt the layers together:

1 Use a walking foot or quilting foot on your machine. Set it up for quilting using decorative thread.

2 You can also hand quilt through all the layers if that is easier or will give you the look that you want.

3 Outline quilting-sew around the shapes.

4 Free motion

5 Grid quilting–(easiest) straight or diagonal lines through all layers

6 Knotting with floss

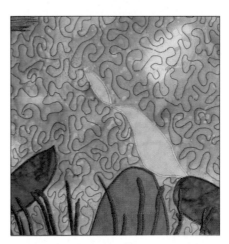

Be sure to return the block on or before the deadline!

Finishing the Block

EMBELLISHING

Use your imagination and supplies on hand to add more dimension and texture to your block—beads, buttons, silk flowers, yarn, etc. Since it is primarily a wall hanging and won't be washed you can use almost anything.

Assembling the Quilt

THE BLOCKS RETURN!

And hopefully they are on time!

Take a finished block and square it up with a ruler and rotary cutter so all are the same size (if needed).

There should be ½" seam allowance but if you cut some off to square it, make sure there is at least ¼" seam allowance all around.

When you have all the blocks, lay them out in order or tape to the wall to make sure you have the entire image properly put together.

First pin the blocks together on seam lines and turn over to check front to see if design lines match up as you want them, if possible.

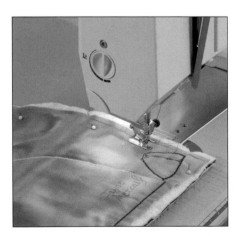

Assemble blocks across one row at a time. With right sides together sew seam.

Next step is to bind all the seams for a clean finish.

HOW TO MAKE BINDING

You will only need binding made of fabric cut on the straight grain since there are no curves when sewing this together. The fabric or color doesn't have to match but it is best to use all cotton fabric to hold a crisp fold when ironed.

CLOVER TAPEMAKER METHOD

The ½" double fold binding is recommended, which is easy to make with a Clover blue #25 tapemaker.

Follow the instructions that come with it. This tool makes it fast and easy to make accurate even binding.

If you don't have a Clover tapemaker, cut fabric into strips that are 2" wide. Press in half lengthwise, then place cut edges into the center fold and press folds with steam until very flat.

Or, you can buy wide double fold bias tape at the fabric stores in basic solid colors. For the seam finishing, the color isn't so important but the perimeter binding that shows on the front should coordinate with the quilt fabrics so you may want to make your own.

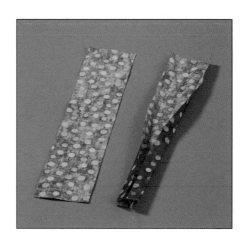

Assembling the Quilt

BINDING THE SEAMS

Open the binding tape, match raw edges so the fold is next to the seam allowance stitching within the seam.

Stitch in the fold.

Fold the tape over the seam and place fold right on seam stitch line.

Stitch close to fold through all layers to enclose the raw edges.

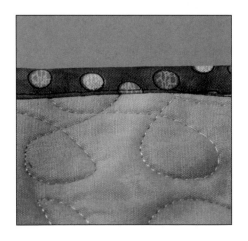

Back view of stitched seam binding.

Sew the rows together pressing the bindings in opposite directions (so the seams aren't too thick) before sewing the rows together.

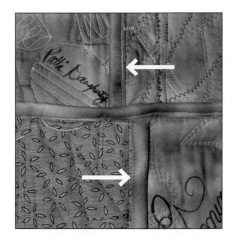

ALTERNATE METHODS:

SERGING THE SEAMS

Instead of sewing binding on all the seams, an easy way would be to use a serger with coordinating color thread. Use a 4-thread overlock.

Also, some sewing machines have an overlock stitch. Try it on a sample and see if you like it. It is not as finished a look as the seam binding.

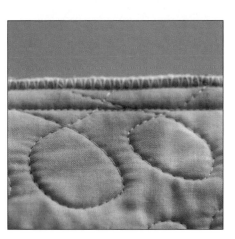

Rod Pocket

1 A rod pocket is attached to the back of the quilt for easy hanging. The fabric used can be the same as the backing fabric or a different piece of the needed size.

Measure the top of the quilt where the rod pocket will be.

Cut the fabric that length by a width of 8½".

2 Press under each short end ¾" to the wrong side and stitch down.

Fold the rod pocket in half lengthwise with wrong sides together and press.

3 Pin the long raw edges to the back at the top of the quilt. The pocket should be about ¾" in from both edges at the sides.

Baste the rod pocket raw edges by machine, less than ¼" from the edge.

The bottom edge of the rod pocket needs to be hand sewn to the backing or tacked to the binding at the seams.

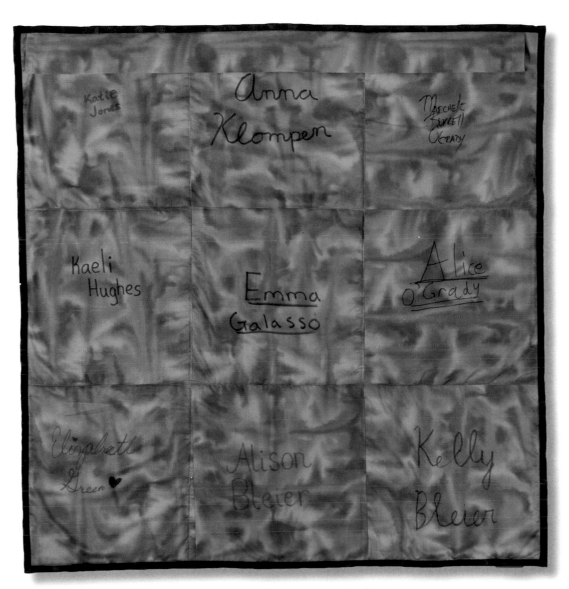

Back of finished
quilt with rod
pocket attached

Binding the outside edges

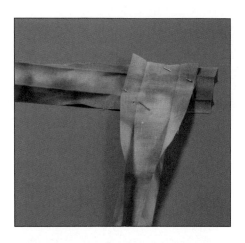

PREPARING THE BINDING

Measure the perimeter of the finished quilt.

Cut and make enough binding to go around it plus an extra 8-10".

To join strips piece them together with a diagonal 45° angle seam. Place one strip horizontal with right side up.

Then place the second strip face down at the end at a right angle and pin.

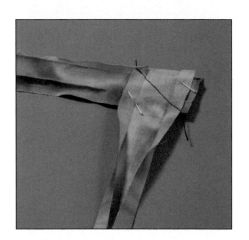

Draw a line from intersecting corner to opposite intersecting corner as in photo.

Sew on that line with a small stitch length (1.8).

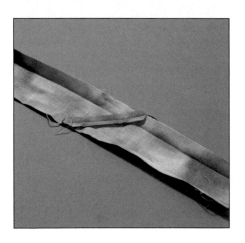

Trim to ¼" and press open.

EASY METHOD

Sew binding across the top of the back as you did for seams. Fold binding over to the front and machine stitch close to the fold. Trim ends even with quilt.

Repeat with binding across the bottom edge.

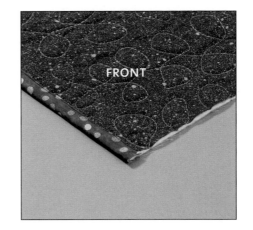

When you sew sides, first turn under ½" at the end of the binding and then sew in fold line. When you get near the end of the quilt, turn under binding ½" so it is even with end of the quilt, sew to end and back stitch.

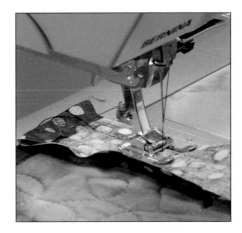

Fold over the binding to the right side and sew close to fold as done previously. To finish, hand stitch the four ends closed with tiny stitches.

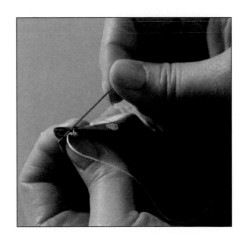

Binding the outside edges

MITERED METHOD

1 Measure the perimeter of the finished quilt and make enough binding plus 8-10" extra. For this method, join all the pieces together in one long continuous strip using the joining method on page 44.

Leaving a 6" tail of binding, start sewing the binding in the middle of one side of the quilt. Align the raw edges of the quilt top with the raw edges of the binding and sew in the fold.

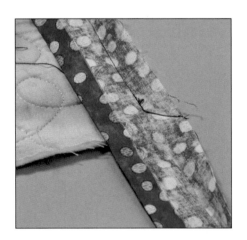

2 If the seam allowance is ½" then stop ½" before the end with the needle in the fabric and raise presser foot and pivot to the corner. Sew to the corner and then take off the machine.

Fold the binding up against this diagonal stitching making a 45 degree angle.

3 Fold the binding back onto itself and align the raw edges of the binding with the new side making sure that the top fold is flush with the top edge of the quilt. Continue to sew in the fold.

4 Repeat for the other corners and continue sewing until you are about 6" away from where you started. Take the beginning tail and fold under a 45 degree angle and press.

Open the end tail out flat. Lay the 45 degree fold on top and draw line on tail following the fold.

5 Then open and put right sides together and pin so fold is along that drawn line and stitch on the line.

Place it back along the edge of the quilt to make sure it is the right length. If too loose, take a little wider seam. Trim seam to ¼" and press open.

Finish sewing the binding to the rest of the quilt edge. Turn the binding over to the front and make sure fold covers the stitching line.

6 Adjust the corners to make neat mitered corners by pressing the fabric into 45 degree corner and pin.

Binding the outside edges

7 Turn the binding over to the front and make sure fold covers the stitching line. You may need to trim 1/8" off the quilt batting sandwich to do this.

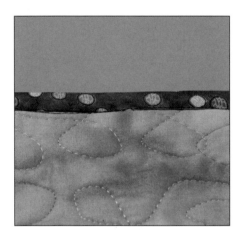

8 Sew close to the fold edge. Photo shows finished binding on the back.

TO HANG YOUR QUILT

Cut a piece of wood 3/8" thick x 2" wide x length of top of quilt less 1". Slip wood through rod pocket and center. Then place on wall and screw the wood ends into the wall. Hold quilt back and don't screw through rod pocket fabric.

Finishing: alternate method

Alternate method used for the girls' flamingo quilt

For the Flamingo quilt the girls didn't quilt their painted blocks with batting and backing. Instead each girl painted on a single layer of fabric for their blocks and then handed them in. They also signed their name on a piece of backing fabric the same size as the block.

Later I squared up the decorated block and the backing piece.

The painted blocks were sewn together to create the picture. The backing squares were pieced so that the names were behind the block that the girls made. They were then layered as in the traditional quilt finishing method with batting between the backing and the top.

It was pinned well all around the outer edges and through the body.

The quilt could then be quilted artistically or machine-stitched, using the easy 'Stitch-in-the-ditch' method, which I did. I stitched exactly on top of the seam so the stitches were invisible. Four lines were stitched in the grid pattern.

Finally, I stitched around the outer edges with long stitches to hold it all together, then proceeded with the rod pocket and edge binding.

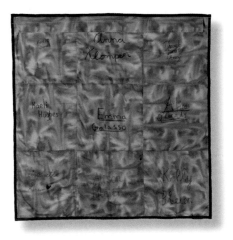

Packet for participants

Now you must prepare a packet of clear information and materials for the participants. Here is a general format geared to adults that quilt, so adjustments would need to be made for a group of children or non-quilters.

Gather all info into some form of container:

- plastic bags
- envelope
- small box
- fancy gift bags that they can keep as souvenir
- plastic folders with closures from office supply store

In the bag will be:

- photo of the entire finished image (unless you want it to be a surprise)
- their cut piece of the image
- Dear Participant letter
- batting- piece one inch bigger all around than desired finished block size
- backing-same size as batting
- instructions for grid method, appliqué, painting and all participant pages copied from this book
- OR a copy of this book!
- instructions on how to layer batting/backing and quilting
- two sheets of acetate
- return envelope addressed to you (optional)
- notions that you may want to provide such as thread, needles, pins (optional)
- postage to return (optional)
- chocolate...it couldn't hurt!

Note: It is assumed the participants will provide fabric to make the block or have paint, markers and fabric to use. If your photo is a 'seascape' for example, it is better NOT to provide the fabric or all the blocks would have the same colors and look too uniform.

Letter to participants

This letter needs to convey what you would like the block maker to do and, hopefully, is thorough enough so they will understand it if you are not actually having a party. Here are some suggestions on what is needed. The quilting stationery on pages 54 and 55 can either be copied or printed from your computer. Go to **www.dragonthreads.com** and use the link to the printable PDF files on the *Quilting Party* page. When using this stationery, please set the margins of your word-processing program to 1.5".

GREETING:

Dear Quilter, Friends of Church, Friends of Mary and Bill.....

WELCOME:

We are so happy that you are willing to participate in making this (charity, gift) quilt for (50th anniversary, church fund-raiser).

INTENT:

It will help raise money for the new playground of our school...addition to our church...
or

We think that this quilt will bring smiles to Mary and Bill for many years and will serve as a great reminder of their first 50 years of marriage...
or

As you know, this May will be Jean's 80th birthday and we would like to present her with a quilt of her family home. We hope that you will participate by making one small 10" square block as part of this quilt!

REQUIREMENTS:

Your 10" (whatever size) block is due back to me by MARCH 15. Please try to get it to me on time or earlier. I will then need time to sew the blocks together, bind all seams, sew the binding around the edges, etc. and have it ready for the celebration.

Instructions are included on the next pages but if you have any questions or problems, please don't hesitate to call or e-mail me. If you don't think you will be able to finish your block on time, please call me as soon as possible so I can arrange a substitute. And don't forget to sign the back of your block.

CLOSING:

Thanks so much for doing this for (Mary and Bill, Lincoln school...). Remember, we need all of you to finish on time or we'll have big holes in the quilt!

Happy Quilting,
name,
address, phone, e-mail

INSTRUCTION SHEET

List the contents of the package and explain the use of each. Include this page in your package.

An example below:

Your kit contains:

- Entire photo-This is what the finished quilt will look like (optional).
- Your slice of the photo to enlarge to a finished size of 10" square.
- Batting- the white felt-like square that goes between the quilt block and the backing.
- Backing - 12" square of yellow fabric.
- Instruction sheets:
    - How to enlarge your photo square
    - Quilting and sewing techniques
    - Non-quilting techniques
    - Finishing your block
    - Making a label
    - Embellishing suggestions
- two acetate sheets for enlarging the photo
- Return envelope

REMEMBER TO RETURN BY _____, PLEASE!

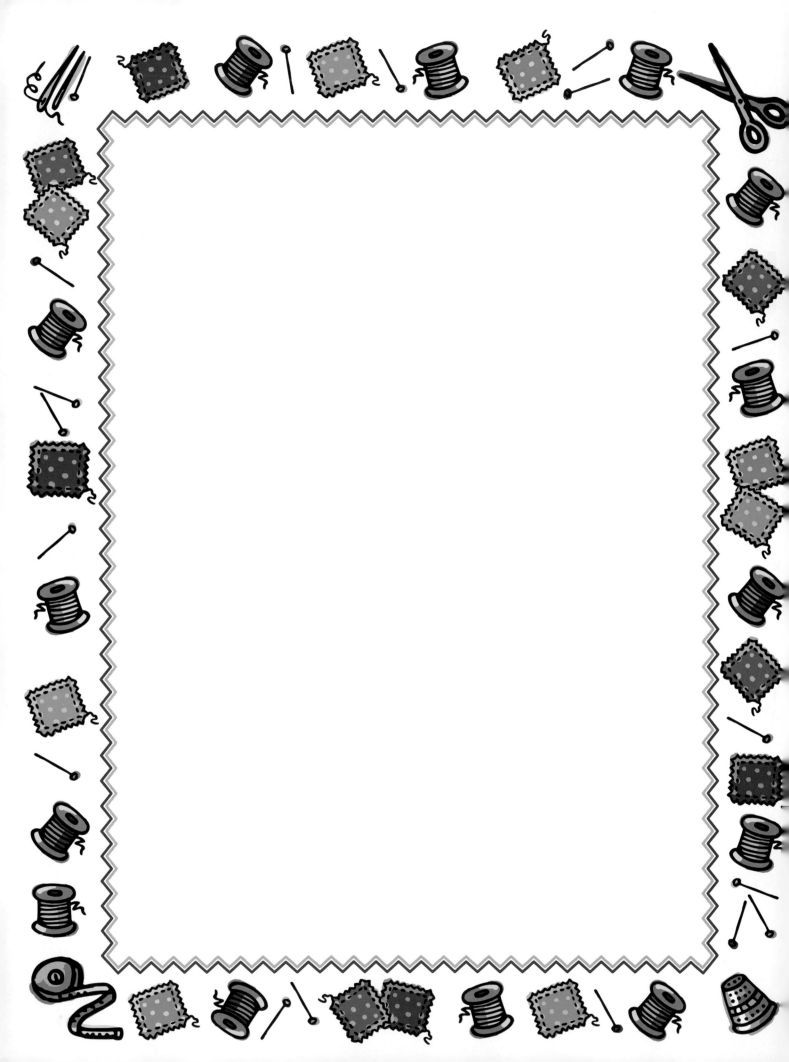

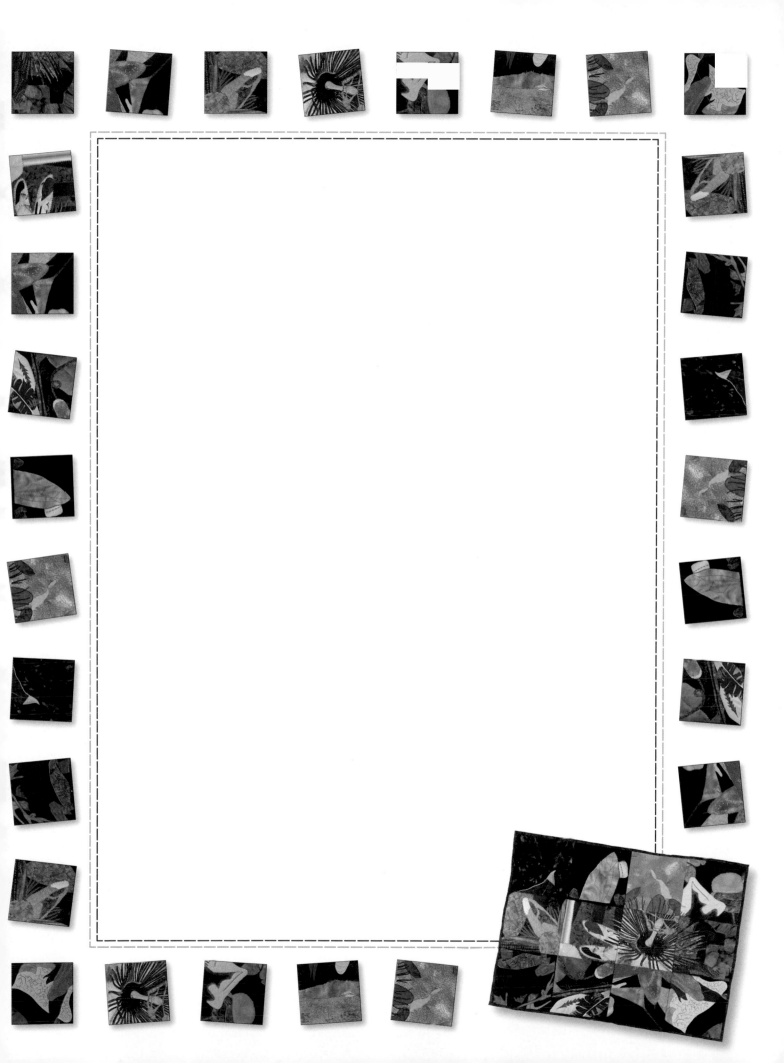

Resources

Many thanks to all the suppliers that provided materials for this book! We had top quality products which made all the difference!

BENARTEX
fabrics
www.benartex.com

BERNINA SEWING MACHINES
www.berninausa.com

BOLD OVER BATIKS
www.boldoverbatiks.com

CLOVER
tape maker, ruler, rotary cutter, mat
www.clover-usa.com

HOBBS BONDED FIBERS
batting
www.hobbsbondedfibers.com

OLFA
rotary cutters, mat, ruler
www.olfa.com

SUPERIOR THREADS
www.superiorthreads.com

TSUKINEKO
Fabrico markers, fabric paints
www.tsukineko.com

YLI THREAD
www.ylicorp.com

STEAM A SEAM 2
transfer adhesive
www.warmcompany.com

BABYLOCK
sewing machines
www.babylock.com

WESTMINSTER FIBERS
fabric
www.westminsterfibers.com

CEDAR CANYON TEXTILES
Paintstiks
www.cedarcanyontextiles.com

JACQUARD CO.
paints, dyes
www.jacquardproducts.com

Thanks to Drew Moffat, the best art teacher ever, for his help with the grid method instructions.

Special thanks to the Quintessential Quilters for their support, especially Kathi Machle and Vicki LaRoche.

Big hugs to Dr. Victoria Rentel for all her beautiful photos that grace these pages and many thanks for all the continued support in all aspects of the book!